Lindsay M. Lyster Writes an Apology Letter

The Father Only Wanted to Protect His Children

From the Liar

Index   **Page**

Chapter 1

Everything going fine with his studies!

In this case, a fine young student was doing fine at his studies at apparently some fly-by night college in Nanaimo, British Columbia, Canada by the name of Malaspina University College.

What is, or what was, Malaspina University College?

As cited, "back in the mid-nineties, the British Columbia Government converted about half dozen community colleges to "university colleges" Malaspina was among them."[1]

Continuing, Malaspina University College, "when approaching private donors or research funding agencies and foundations, Malaspina has to begin its presentation with a lengthy explanations of what a university college is."[2]

Was Malaspina University College doing well?

Apparently not, as cited, "Malaspina expects to offer significantly fewer courses this fall. The Malaspina Faculty Association has learned that layoff notices will be going out on Monday morning to 15 employees at Malaspina. While the Faculty Association is working with management at Malaspina University-College and is hopeful that layoffs can be rescinded, if these cuts are not reversed, they will likely result in the end of degree programs in Computer Science and Earth Sciences."[3]

As cited, 'the hardest hit department is Computer Science where - including the cuts last year - the department has been cut in half. "Cuts of this magnitude mean the immediate elimination of the Computer Science diploma program," said Dominique Roelants, the most senior member of the Computer Science Department and also a senior member of the Malaspina Faculty Association Executive".'[4]

In one blog, it was asked: "is Vancouver Island University (formerly Malaspina University-College) a good university to study MBA? I'm living outside Canada and applying as international student. I was wondering if anyone can help me and giving me idea regarding this university."[5]

The reply: "Vancouver island university is not a good university for MBA... Most Canadian's have never heard of that place... To find the best university that suits you, I suggest you borrow an issue of Macleans for the November issue, where they have the MBA university rankings in Canada."[6]

Intrigued, the author examined what students were saying about the "professors" at Malaspina University-College (a.k.a. Vancouver Island university).

Just a quick look at "professors" beginning with the letter "c" in the field of business found some not too flattering comments:

As cited, for professor Joseph Chang from the Business Department, one student recorded this comment "This teacher is not what ppl expect to see in MBA program. He doesn't know SIMPLES things (starting from geography). He lacks grammar and classes are useless. Just simply reading the book would help more."[7]

For another professor by the name of Patrick Chuankamnerdkarn, again in the Department of Business, one student had this to say "the Worst "professor" (I'm not sure if I should call him professor) I ever had. Treat students as small kids, doesn't care about your opinion or idea. TO AVOID!!!"[8]

Another professor, in Marketing, by the name of Patrick Chuankarn, one student had this to say "It is nuts to let someone that cannot speak English properly (confuses singular/plural, past/present/future etc.) How does the University expect students to learn and or continue to use the language properly if the teacher cannot!!! What the hell happened to standards??? Why are people let into the U. that cannot even pass grade 3 English???"[9]

Another professor, in Accounting, by the name of Stew Churlish, one student had this to say "I'm sure he is very good at accounting, but he is definitely not cut out to be a teacher. He often made mistakes and most of the class could not follow his scattered instruction. He solves problems on the board without instructing on how it is done. He was often corrected by the students on mistakes he made."[10]

And one last professor, in Management, by the name of Dana Collette was cited by one student as "Probably one of the worst profs I had in VIU. After finishing her course I feel as if I haven't learned much, if anything I'm just more confused. Didn't appreciate her teaching techniques, her interpersonal manner towards students or the way she built her exams. God awful. Now hopefully won't have to deal with her again."[11]

Interestingly, all these professors, except one, are still working at Malaspina University-College (a.k.a. Vancouver Island university) as per the school's Employee Directory checked on 04 May 2011.

Apparently, Malaspina University-College (a.k.a. Vancouver Island university) doesn't give much credence to student comments, such as "He lacks grammar and classes are useless. Just simply reading the book would help more" or "He was often corrected by the students on mistakes he made" or "Probably one of the worst profs I had in VIU"?

Well, if Malaspina University-College (a.k.a. Vancouver Island university) isn't apparently very good at business, what programs were noted on the internet about this place?[12]

How about hair Styling?

The author found this glowing report about Malaspina University College: "I received my training at Malaspina University College and have been in the hair industry since 1994."

Yep, what a college – the serious subjects appear to be "crap" yet the "trades" are fine?

Footnotes

1. Canadian Universities Forum

2. What it Means to be a University

3 - 4. Axe Falls at Malaspina University College

5 - 6. Best Answer - Chosen by Asker

7 - 11. Rate my professors

12. bios - Paris Styling Group - Where Passion fuels Success
Duncan, British Columbia

Chapter 2

What did other student say about professors?

Disturbed about the comments about professors at Malaspina University-College (a.k.a. Vancouver Island university) in the field of business, in the previous chapter, the author took a synopsis of student comments regarding professors in other departments at this place.

As recorded, virtually every department at Malaspina University-College (a.k.a. Vancouver Island University) was spanned!

In Accounting, one student cited this about professor Patricia Adam ""She should stick to running Ricky's restaurant. She quite often cannot answer questions and says "I can't do it" or "Don't ask me how I got this". Not lenient with extensions even if you are willing to get docked late marks. She doesn't explain things well and this is the first class I may potentially fail and I blame her"[1]

In Geography, one student had this to say about professor Don Alexander "Horrible teacher! Always shows up late, doesn't teach anything just relies on the class to teach everything for him through presentations. If you can avoid taking a class with him then avoid him Weak with marks too will give a grade with no basis or actual mark attached so you don't know if it's a high A or low and can't figure out your final grade."[2]

In Education, one student cited this about professor Kerry Armstrong "She's been fired. That's how negative her response was. She taught us nothing about assessment and evaluation! The faculty had to put together a series of workshops out of our regular class time to catch us up! HORRIBLE!"[3]

In English, one student had this to say about professor Anna Atkinson "She is an extreme radical feminist, beware. Her marking is disgusting-totally low grades no matter what. She wasted my time. She is an ok person but a crappy teacher."[4]

In Philosophy, one student cited this about professor Jim Ayers "I found it extremely difficult to understand him, especially in class due to mumbling and illegible handwriting. He often doesn't say all that he thinks while explaining something, so you only get half the story, very annoying and very confusing. Don't recommend this guy at all."[5]

In Creative Writing & Journalism, one student had this to say about professor Rhonda Bailey "When asked what we could do we were told "Find something to do" Most boring class I've ever had, it's a challenge just to stay awake."[6]

In Child & Youth, one student cited this about professor Robert Bates "Beware! He is very unprofessional, unorganized and very self-absorbed.... avoid his classes, you will be happy you did."[7]

In Social Work, one student had this to say about professor Bonnie-Jean Buffie "Brings her personal issues into her work. Her attempts at "being fair" only work if it's convenient or okay to her, again bringing in her personal stuff. She favours particular students, even though they do not do the work, they just put on a good act, and kiss up - apparently speaking your mind and challenging stuff is frowned upon."[8]

In Hospitality, one student cited this about professor Stephen Burr "Unclear expectations for projects, little to no guidance throughout the course - yet marks as if there has been. Not very fair, would not take another class with him again."[9]

In Law, one student had this to say about professor Dana Chamberlain "The worst class I've ever taken... labs were confusing she wasn't helpful in explaining them at all. Class was dry and boring. Just as useful to sit at home and read the textbook. Crappy"[10]

In Ethnic Studies, one student cited this about professor Laura Cranmer "Confusing classes, instructor is always flustered, directions are unclear, but a stickler for rules for students, tough marker when assignments are ambiguous."[11]

In English, one student had this to say about professor Marcia Crosby "WORST PROFESSOR EVER! OMFG where to start!? She's late, arrogant, and ignorant, talked about herself way too much, wouldn't let anyone use a laptop in class, had spelling mistakes in her syllabus, for AN ENGLISH CLASS!! Altogether useless, and because I took her course in the summer I couldn't get my money back!! DO NOT TAKE HER CLASS!!!!"[12]

In Sociology, one student cited this about professor Linda Dersken "Seriously, I cannot believe she gets paid to do nothing! Class content fairly boring, Linda barely taught anything in class, and missed about a third of the course. Complete waste of time and money."[13]

In Chemistry, one student had this to say about professor Peter Diamente "Horrible... That is all I have to say."[14]

In Fisheries Biology, one student cited this about professor Stefanie Duff "Terrible; worst prof I've ever had so far. Her lecture notes make no sense. I had to research the material on my own through Wikipedia. Some of the emails she sends to the class are condescending; she treats us like children. I would never take another class from her again."[15]

In Nursing, one student had this to say about professor Lori Evans "Lori has missed classes to pursue her political agenda and we now have spent the rest of the semester playing catch-up. In response to any question students ask to try to gain clarity in this now messy and rushed semester; Lori's response is 'this is adult learning'."[16]

In Nursing, one student cited this about professor Debbie Freeborn "I didn't learn a thing! Emphasised trivial things. Could have used our time better by teaching more important things."[17]

In Nursing again, another student had this to say about professor Julie Gibler "Worst teacher I've ever had. Her classes are ridiculously boring and her exams are incomprehensible. Our class started off as majority A student, our class average for our patho final was 60% not because we are stupid but because the exam was stupid!!! If you can, switch out of her class ASAP!"[18]

In Hospitality, one student cited this about professor Kathleen Haggith "Egotistical I felt sorry for the students with disabilities in her classroom. More concerned with fashion and material goods than the education or esteem of her students, perhaps she would be more at home teaching economics. Not a good person in my opinion."[19]

Wow?

"Not a good person in my opinion."[20]

In Nursing, one student had this to say about professor Nancy Hendry, "Nancy is a bit of two worlds one day she is your best friend caring nurturing and absolutely a riot. The next minute she is screaming at you and cutting you down in front of the whole class" and another student said this, "I've never been treated more like a child... even in Elementary school! She is VERY knowledgable, but her teaching methods are crude and RUDE. She pick certain people in the class to demean (Usually a struggling, unpopular student)... Seemingly to see if she can get this student to drop out! Shameful!"[21]

Another student in Accounting had this to say about professor Jim Hughes, "Absolutely horrible teacher. Regurgitating another teachers work. Barely understands what he is supposed to be teaching. Every deadline got extended. Did not even know how to use the program that we were supposed to be learning" and another student said this, "Worst teacher I've ever had. Half of the course was supposed to be about simply accounting but it seemed like he had never used it before."[22]

One student had this to say about Business professor Chris Jaeger, "Did not like his teaching methods. He gave us a seating plan in university... kinda ridiculous. He is a VERY hard marker and favours his favorite students. He is very frustrating to deal with. I have avoided him at all costs since this course."[23]

Incredibly, as per the Employee Directory for this school checked on 04 May, 2011 all these professors are still working at Malaspina University-College (a.k.a. Vancouver Island university), except for three?

Apparently, again, Malaspina University-College (a.k.a. Vancouver Island university) gives no credence to a preponderance of student protestations about the quality of teaching, such as "Horrible teacher! Always shows up late, doesn't teach anything just relies on the class to teach everything for him through presentations" or "Most boring class I've ever had, it's a challenge just to stay awake" or "She favours particular students - apparently speaking your mind and challenging stuff is frowned upon" or "Confusing classes, instructor is always flustered, directions are unclear" or "WORST PROFESSOR EVER! OMFG where to start!? She's late, arrogant, and ignorant" or "Horrible... That is all I have to say."

Anyone want to attend Malaspina University-College (a.k.a. Vancouver Island university) after reading these deplorable comments about its professors by students?

Footnotes

1 - 20. *Rate my professor*

Chapter 3

The professor who lied!

As mentioned in Chapter 1, a fine young student was doing fine at his studies at Malaspina University College in Nanaimo, British Columbia, Canada.

That is, until the day one of his professors lied?

What?

With the deplorable comments by students about Malaspina University College [a.k.a. Vancouver Island University] in the previous chapter, anything seems possible.

But, a lying professor?

What was that all about?

It all started in November, 2005 when Malaspina University College "professor" Helen Brown in the History Department wrote on one of this young fellow's papers "an important part of preparing for the final exam is attending class. You have missed 10 of 19 classes in addition to arriving 50 minutes late for another" [see Appendix 1].

Well, for one, the boy's father knew full-well that this was an outright lie because he was retired and drove his son to Malaspina University College.

The boy's father knew full-well that his son had not missed 10 of 19 classes and he was never 50 minutes late for a class.

When this a fine young student confronted this liar of a professor on 10th November, this Malaspina University College "professor" Helen Brown retracted her "estimate" downward to something more approaching the truth [see Appendix 2a & 2b]

This interaction is referred to in a letter dated 24th November, 2005 written by the boy's father to the Dean of Arts and Humanities, Steven M. Lane, at this Malaspina University College about this liar of a "professor". The letter speaks for itself, and appears in Appendix 2a and 2b.

What did this liar of a "professor" do in a vindictive reaction to the father's letter written 24th November, 2005 complaining about "professor" Helen Brown initial lie – she repeated her lie on the boy's final written assignment for her History 476 class presented to her on 24th November and returned to the boy later [see Appendix 3].

As appearing in Appendix 3, this liar of a professor, again stated "You were absent for many classes and that impacts on your participation grade" [see Appendix 3].

Chapter 4

The professor who also appeared paranoid?

This Malaspina University College "professor" Helen Brown in the History Department, cited in the previous chapter, in addition to her false statements mentioned in that chapter also appeared to be somewhat paranoid.

When the father wrote an email dated 17 October 2005 to this "professor" on behalf of his son who was sick [see Appendix 4], she did not reply.

As you can see, the email from the father was straight forward and polite [see Appendix 4].

The next day, as cited in the father's email he saw this so-called "professor" with his son who had gotten out of his sick-bed to see her.

The father followed this meeting with a follow-up email dated 18 October 2005 [see Appendix 5].

As you can see, the email from the father was again straight forward and polite [see Appendix 5].

How did "professor" Helen Brown react to these two simple emails?

With apparent absolute paranoia?

Unknown to the father or his son, this "professor" Helen Brown wrote an email dated 19 October 2005 to the Dean of Arts and Humanities, Steven M. Lane [see Appendix 6a and 6b]?

In it, "professor" Helen Brown writes "I have never heard of a parent acting as a proxy and whether such a thing exists at Malaspina" [see Appendix 6a and 6b]?

What?

This "professor" Helen Brown has never heard of a parent writing a note for a sick child?

This "professor" Helen Brown has never heard of a spouse or loved-one writing a note for a partner who is sick?

Why would "professor" Helen Brown write such an email?

It surely isn't for the reasons she mentions further in her email dated 19 April where she says "it is in my student's best interests that we deal directly with each other" [see Appendix 6a and 6b]?

We have already seen in the previous chapter how "professor" Helen Brown deals with her student(s), she lies [see Appendix 1, 2a and 2b, and 3]?

Is it because she wanted no interference from an out-side source when she lied [see Appendix 1, 2a and 2b, and 3]?

With the comments about the so-called "professors" at Malaspina University-College (a.k.a. Vancouver Island university) appearing in Chapter 2, anything appears possible?

After all, the proxy note seems straight-forward too [see Appendix 7a and 7b].

Footnote

Refer to Helen Brown's comment in Appendix 6a, "the discussion was amiable and the parent left the building." This statement will be important later in this book.

Chapter 5

The vice-president of student services!

Incredibly, this wasn't the end of the paranoia at Malaspina University-College (a.k.a. Vancouver Island University)?

As cited by Patrick Ross, the vice-president of student services, in a memorandum dated 14 January 2009 he makes reference to the following:

> 3.　　　　　As Vice-President of Student Services, my responsibilities included investigating incidents relating to Malaspina's academic and code of conduct policies. In this regard, I first became aware that the Complainant was the father of two Malaspina students in the Autumn of 2005 when I received notice from Dr. Steven Lane, the Dean of Malaspina's Arts and Humanities department, that one of his professors, Professor Helen Brown, was concerned about the Complainant's attempt to act as a "proxy" for his two adult children who were both students in one of her history courses. Attached to this my Affidavit and marked as Exhibit "A" is a true copy of a memorandum addressed to Steven Lane from Helen Brown dated October 19, 2005.

This email dated 19 October 2005 by "professor" Helen Brown to the Dean of Arts and Humanities, Steven M. Lane appear as Appendix 6a and 6b.

Chapter 6

The dean of arts and humanities!

As cited by Patrick Ross, the vice-president of student services, in a memorandum dated 14 January 2009 he also makes reference to the following:

> 5.　　　　Attached to this my Affidavit and marked as Exhibit "C" is an annotated e-mail message from Steven Lane to me dated November 30, 2005 relating to Professor Brown's further concerns about dealing with the Complainant as a representative for his two children. I believe that the handwritten notes on the bottom of the e-mail message are by one of the instructors.

This email dated 30 November 2005 by the Dean of Arts and Humanities Steven Lane appears as Appendix 8a and 8b.

The most important line in this email dated 30 November 2005 by the Dean of Arts and Humanities Steven Lane is the statement "Helen (Brown) is also worried about the father showing up in a belligerent, threatening manner again" [see Appendix 8a and 8b]?

What? As the father said, what is this lying "wack-jack" talking about?

Didn't "professor" Helen Brown just say in an earlier email dated dated 19 October 2005 to the Dean of Arts and Humanities, Steven M. Lane that "the discussion was amiable and the parent left the building" [see Appendix 6a]?

Who is lying here?

Is it "professor" Helen Brown when she verbally speaks to the Dean of Arts and Humanities, Steven M. Lane?

Or, is it the Dean of Arts and Humanities, Steven M. Lane, when he wrote his email dated 30 November 2005 to Patrick Ross, the vice-president of student services?

As the father said, one of these two birds is lying?

Or, as the father said, maybe both are lying? A conspiracy?

Chapter 7

The vice-president of student services again!

Did Patrick Ross, the vice-president of student services, also apparently join the conspiracy?

As the father said, you bet he did?

In a big way?

After all, it was Patrick Ross, the vice-president of student services, who severed the father's "proxy" on 01 August 2006 with respect to his children – most likely as the father was not about to let lies perpetuate by the so-called professors at Malaspina University-College (a.k.a. Vancouver Island university) – see "professor" Helen Brown's false statements [see Appendix 1, 2a and 2b, and 3].

Nor the lie appearing in the email dated 30 November 2005 by the Dean of Arts and Humanities Steven Lane [Appendix 8a and 8b], where Steven Lane falsely states "Helen (Brown) is also worried about the father showing up in a belligerent, threatening manner again".

As stated by the father, one of these two birds is lying?

As mentioned, didn't "professor" Helen Brown just say in an earlier email dated dated 19 October 2005 to the Dean of Arts and Humanities, Steven M. Lane that "the discussion was amiable and the parent left the building" [see Appendix 6a]?

Again, is it "professor" Helen Brown who lied when she verbally spoke to the Dean of Arts and Humanities, Steven M. Lane?

Or, is it the Dean of Arts and Humanities, Steven M. Lane, when he wrote his email dated 30 November 2005 to Patrick Ross, the vice-president of student services?

Or, as mentioned, maybe both are lying?

A conspiracy?

Where did this Patrick Ross, the vice-president of student, fit into this conspiracy?

Well, let's see.

Based on the lies in the Dean of Arts and Humanities, Steven M. Lane, email dated 30 November 2005, where this Steven Lane makes this false statement "Helen (Brown) is also worried about the father showing up in a belligerent, threatening manner again" Patrick Ross, the vice-president of student services revokes the father's proxy status and actually bars the father from campus?

What?

The father tries to protect his children from lies by the so-called professors at Malaspina University-College (a.k.a. Vancouver Island University) as well as the lie in Dean of Arts and Humanities, Steven M. Lane, email dated 30 November 2005 and he is barred from campus?

And, now for the biggest lie of all – one by Patrick Ross, the vice-president of student services, who under oath lied!

You see, the father who suffers from PTSD, was waiting in his vehicle while his children paid their fees or something like that and he was quietly listening to some music when he was approached by "some guy".

As the father said, the guy was shouting and gesturing wildly with his arms?

The guy came up to the vehicle and pounded on the window, like some wild lunatic – shouting and screaming?

When the lunatic moved away, the father got out of the vehicle and said "what are you ranting about moron" or words to that effect?

As cited in a memo dated 21 November, 2007 "this guy" [turns out to be Patrick Ross, the vice-president of student services] confirmed this interaction [see Appendix 9].

The father complained to the British Columbia Human Rights Department that he was being denied public access under his PSTD disability.

"This guy" [Patrick Ross, the vice-president of student services] outright lied under oath in his deposition to the British Columbia Human Rights Department where he stated he did not bang on the vehicle window [see Appendix 10a and 10b].

As such, he apparently committed perjury?

Isn't that what it's called when one lies under oath?

Hence, the college protected the lying "professor" at any cost – even apparently committing perjury in the process?

Chapter 8

The vindictive college!

What did this "great" college [Malaspina University-College (a.k.a. Vancouver Island university)] do when it found out the young student was working on campus in security to help pay for his education?

Vindictively, it asked his employer Footprints Security that this young student be taken off the roster working at Malaspina University-College (a.k.a. Vancouver Island University)?

What?

Who did this?

Was it that "wack-jack" Patrick Ross [as the father calls him], the vice-president of student services who outright lied under oath in his deposition to the British Columbia Human Rights Department [see Appendix 10a and 10b]?

Chapter 9

Possibly one of the worst colleges?

As far as the young fellow's father is concerned – it has to be one of the worst colleges in Canada, if not the world.

And, from the comments by more students attending this college, the father may be correct in his impressions of Malaspina University-College (a.k.a. Vancouver Island University).

As further cited, one student had this to say about professor Lev Idels in the Mathematics Department, "Would highly recommend not taking his class. He does not explain questions well and does not take questions. Quite rude and makes assumptions on your work ethic due to his poor teaching and organization. STAY AWAY take Dave's class instead or your GPA will hate you for it!!"[1]

Another student reported that professor Rob Jeacock in Economics was a "BAD PROFESSOR!!!! Do NOT take any classes from him. He expects students to know all terms and concepts even before they've read the first page of the text. His examples are incomprehensible and his tests are unnecessarily difficult. They do not contain the information he teaches in class, but things we didn't even learn. BE AWARE. DO NOT TAKE HIM!!"[2]

Another student reported that professor Rosmy Jean-Louis, again in Economics, wrote "Probably one of the most confusing prof's I've ever had. He is very unclear on the points he's trying to make. He tells us to read the text book, then teaches us stuff completely different from the book. He is extremely hard to understand, and when you ask him to use or do an example, he gets frustrated and yells at you. NOT A COOL PROF!"[3]

Another student wrote this about professor Ruth Kirson in Psychology, "If you take this class you just have to read the text book and not attend class. Her tests have no relevance to notes that you will take in class. It's very frustrating. I advise anyone who wished to have an enthusiastic teacher, don't take Ruth. If you are a textbook enthusiast, take Ruth. It's a lot of information rather than learning."[4]

Another student wrote this about professor Richard Lane in the English Department "Erratic teaching style. Demanding and unwilling to help his students. Incredibly mean" followed by another student that said "Horrible teacher, so strict and very demanding for a first year course. Expects way too much and grades way too hard. Never hated an English class until i went into his class, and I have never failed an essay until his class. Avoid him!"[5]

Professor Mary Lindsay in the Education Department was described this way by one student "Class was ridiculous. I'm glad it's over and she enjoyed watching us struggle" and by another student this way "Hated this class. She is unclear in her expectations and runs around in circles when she is asked questions. When going to see her about assignments PRE-hand in, she says they are great. Then she marks you incredibly low on the final product, AFTER she said it was good. Never want to take a class with her again."[6]

Another professor, Hui "Joy" Liu, in Economics was described as "Joy seemed uninterested in teaching the class. She would come to class and just read off of the poorly put together slides. She was also hard to understand with her thick accent and poor English. I would avoid taking another class by her" and by another student "Joy was easily one of the worst profs I have ever had. I get a headache trying to understand what she's saying. The outlines of her courses leave you going into the exam with 70% of your grade unknown and her tests are only 30 MC and do not give you an accurate measure of how you are doing in her class. She is an AWFUL instructor."[7]

Computer Science fared no better, with one student saying this about professor Sarath Jayewaderna, "The class was horrible. The prof. didn't consider our computer abilities prior to teaching us. He believed we all knew a lot about computers. The notes were confusing and had too much info. The tests weren't even written by him. He asked for feed-back but did not apply it. He blamed us for a low grade instead of evaluating his teaching abilities."[8]

What about Mathematics? According to one student, professor Djun Kim "shows up to class late and then tells you to do questions from the textbook. There's no teaching involved. If you struggle at math never take his course he can't help you."[9]

Economics professor Mark Loken was described by one

student as, "He drifts away from economics and swims in a world of his own. Terrible teacher, terrible communication techniques, talk solely about the fact that he hates his brother, hates milk and love beer. Oh, and he has a thing for BC ferries I would assume. Avoid at all costs, I got ripped off, he should be fired ASAP...Simply disgusted when I think of econ."[10]

Here's quite a comment about Education professor Virginia MacCarthy, "This prof should really retire. She thinks everyone is out to get her. Don't bother arguing a point, she is always right. The book walk, is more like an afternoon nap. She is awesome at teaching potential colleagues "what not to do"! Treated us like we were kindergartners."[11]

No better for this Business "prof", one student described Mike MacColl as, "He is the worst prof of VIU. He is useless, helpless, rude, arrogant prof so be careful students don't waste your time and money in his class. You can nothing expect something good from him. He has no hesitation to give you F grade. Stay away from MaCcoll as possible and drop that course which is taught by MaCcoll. Save your money, time and future" while another student said, "He's the worst! Seriously! You never know what to expect! If you are not a gray mouse you are in trouble! He might (!) like you if you are quiet and always agree with him and can stand his **** and other jokes. But he might as well not. And this had NOTHING to do with your performance in the class!"[12]

What about Music, one student had this to say about professor Collin MacQuarrie, "Needs help with his social graces...and needs to learn how to have a course/lesson plan...always late with music, and when you ask for help on the computer he shows you the manual."[13]

English professor Jeannie Martin fared no better, with one student saying "She is very difficult and picky professor. I spent all my time to finish and revise my paper, but I still got F. I will never take her any classes any more" with another following with "This woman is condescending, and often intimidating. While she may be knowledgeable, she was reluctant to give advice. Her lectures were often overtly opinionated, and noticeably strident. She had little time for differing opinions, and quite frequently refused to entertain them. Hard work was no guaranty of success. First Years Beware."[14]

For Nursing professor Patricia Meyer, one student wrote "She acts unprofessional while telling us to be professional. Talks down to other staff members because she thinks she's better than everyone else. She's controlling and has to have everything done her way."[15]

Business professor Vanessa Oltmann was described this way by one student, "Yikes! Extremely boring/hard to understand lectures. She has a monotone voice that will put you to sleep. Accounting is hard enough to get through, she does not help. Doesn't really teach hard problems well, so if you take her be prepared to put a lot of work in to get through the course and ask for outside help."[16]

One student described Education professor Heather Pastro as, "Heather sucked. She was unclear about EVERYTHING. Last time I checked I was attending university NOT preschool; collages and show n' tell are a waste of my time, which is what we ended up doing in class. And she wonders why I didn't go. Come on. Funny thing is I'm an A student and I received a C in her class, enough said. Waste of time. Run fast."[17]

Another Education professor Nancy Randall was described as "Snippy, petty and vindictive."[18]

Recreation, Parks and Tourism professor David Robinson was described this way by one student, "Well what can I say, he had a personal grudge against half the class, the only marks you get are either an A or an F and he likes to play favorites. If you're not on his good side right away, then look out because he will go out of his way to make sure your life is horrible!"[19]

Computer Science professor Dominique Roelants was described by one student as, "Rude and acts like a know-it all. Bad teacher, never take a class with him again" and by another student as, "A really bad teacher. Unclear in lecture. He seems never care how student does."[20]

As for Business professor Ian Ross, one student describes him as, "One word! RUN!!! The WORST teacher of my LIFE. He talks only about him way too into himself. Just a blob who makes school a living hell for you."[20]

Another student had this to say about Social Work professor Heather Sanrud, "Terrible, terrible, terrible! Keep away from this one."[21]

Physics/Engineering/Astronomy professor Eric Smiley was described as "Maybe a good engineer in the field but he can NOT teach. NEVER take his courses" by one student.[22]

One student described Education professor Neil Smith as "Unorganized goof. Assignments are a mess and instruction is all over the map. In the end, feed the monkey his sh*t and move on to the next class."[23]

One student had this to say about professor Don Stone in the Geography department "I have only had Don for one class, but it he was a very difficult instructor. He speaks very quickly and interrogates students while they are madly writing notes and expects an answer right away. He does not give part marks - either right or wrong. I took another prereq for my major through an online university to avoid him. Kills the GPA" while another had this to say, "I agree with the cheese grater guy!! AVOID HIM TO KEEP YOUR GPA UP!!!"[24]

English professor Craig Tapping was referred to as "Dr. T is pompous & rejoices in his glory days of teaching @ UBC & this & that. He DOES have favs, even though he will tell you he does not. My class began with 35 ppl & finished with 10!" and by another student as "Crazy as they come, all I remember is he seemed like a champ at first, but once it came out that he still lives with his mother and his outrageous marking scheme . . . I lost all respect for this character. Be warned he takes interest in 5 people per class, if you're not a part of those 5 - drop the class IMMEDIATELY!!"[25]

One student said this about Management professor Frank Theuerkorn "I can honestly say Frank is the worst instructor I've ever had. His slides are unintelligible. Some of his information (horticulture) is inaccurate or speculation but he's pompous and arrogant so there's never discussion. His grading is imaginative and his assignments are unclear", while another student said "He gives no clear expectations for assignments and has questionable marking. Worst class I've ever taken, by far. Avoid at all costs", and finally one student simply said "don't waste your time."[26]

Education professor Jean Tonski was described by one student as "She has an incredibly un-engaging teaching style- always a random rant. Always unprepared and disorganized, however everyone gets a good mark" and by another student as "Nothin' but bad experiences with this one."[27]

Forest Resources professor Michel Vallee was described by one student as "Absolutely terrible. Does not explain how he wants things then gets mad when it's not what he wants. Never there, unclear, unhappy, waste of time."[28]

Mathematics professor Julian West was described by one student as "If you are in a class with Julian West get out before it is too late. He is not clear at all, very disorganized and mean. You will be made fun of if you ask any questions in this class. He spends way too much time on easy stuff and when it gets hard he skips over it. He has class favourites, all young girls, otherwise he doesn't care how you do."[29]

Ethnic Studies professor Joyce White was described by one student as "Cannot seem to explain assignments with any consistency. Scrambled lectures."[30]

One student described Nursing professor Carrie Willekes as "This nursing instructor is the worst. She talks down to students and gives them**** because they don't know something right in front of the patients."[31]

So?

Apparently, are many of the professors at Malaspina University-College (a.k.a. Vancouver Island university) just plain "crappy" according to many students?

Anyone want to attend Malaspina University-College (a.k.a. Vancouver Island university) after reading these deplorable comments about its professors by students?

Incredibly, as per the Employee Directory for this school checked on 04 May, 2011 all these professors are still working at Malaspina University-College (a.k.a. Vancouver Island university), except for seven?

Apparently, again, Malaspina University-College (a.k.a. Vancouver Island university) gives no credence to a preponderance of student protestations about the quality of teaching, such as "Would highly recommend not taking his class. STAY AWAY" or "Erratic teaching style. Demanding and unwilling to help his students" or "Class was ridiculous. I'm glad it's over" or "Hated this class. She is unclear in her expectations and runs around in circles when she is asked questions" or

"He drifts away from economics and swims in a world of his own. Terrible teacher" or "This prof should really retire. She thinks everyone is out to get her" or "Well what can I say, he had a personal grudge against half the class … he likes to play favorites. If you're not on his good side right away, then look out because he will go out of his way to make sure your life is horrible!"

It also appears that some are outright liars?

As, are apparently some of the management?

Any want to attend this place?

Footnotes

1 - 31. *Rate my professor*

Chapter 10

Why would a college feel free to outright lie?

Why would a college feel free to outright lie?

As mentioned in Chapter 6, Patrick Ross, the vice-president of student services, in a memorandum dated 14 January 2009 made reference to the following:

> 5.   Attached to this my Affidavit and marked as Exhibit "C" is an annotated e-mail message from Steven Lane to me dated November 30, 2005 relating to Professor Brown's further concerns about dealing with the Complainant as a representative for his two children. I believe that the handwritten notes on the bottom of the e-mail message are by one of the instructors.

This email dated 30 November 2005 by the Dean of Arts and Humanities Steven Lane appears as Appendix 8a and 8b.

The most important line in this email dated 30 November 2005 by the Dean of Arts and Humanities Steven Lane is the statement "Helen (Brown) is also worried about the father showing up in a belligerent, threatening manner again" [see Appendix 8a and 8b]?

What?

As also mentioned in Chapter 6, as the father said, what is this lying "wack-jack" talking about?

Didn't "professor" Helen Brown just say in an earlier email dated dated 19 October 2005 to the Dean of Arts and Humanities, Steven M. Lane that "the discussion was amiable and the parent left the building" [see Appendix 6a]?

As the father said, who is lying here?

Is it "professor" Helen Brown when she verbally speaks to the Dean of Arts and Humanities, Steven M. Lane?

Or, is it the Dean of Arts and Humanities, Steven M. Lane, when he wrote his email dated 30 November 2005 to Patrick Ross, the vice-president of student services?

As the father said, one of these two birds is lying?

Or, as the father said, maybe both are lying?

A conspiracy?

Yes, probably?

And, why would that occur?

Did the College know that British Columbia Human Rights would do nothing about their unethical behavior?

Chapter 11

Let's see how others fared with complaints against the University?

As cited, "Vancouver Island University has lost an appeal of a small claims court decision that means it must now pay an international student $7,500 plus $700 for his court costs."[1]

What?

The details, as reported, "Avanish Kumar, from India, sued the former Malaspina University-College last year after he was refused entry into a prerequisite program in the summer of 2007 for the MBA course starting in October 2007 and VIU would not refund his initial $10,000 payment."[2]

What?

Apparently, the prerequisite program may have been for "students without an undergraduate degree in business complete an additional 2 month Foundation program before the start of the MBA program."[3]

Yet, what does this Vancouver Island University do – apparently refuse the guy entry into a pre-requisite program and then try to keep his fees besides?

As the father said, is this some sort of shyster outfit?

As further reported, "Kumar had expected to start the program in October 2007 and when he instead asked to be refunded the $10,000 he paid to confirm his place in the program, that was refused."[4]

"Kumar testified that he wanted his money back so that he could apply to BCIT."[5]

VIU also tried to argue that Kumar's application was a "ruse" to get into Canada and that he never wanted to attend classes at VIU.[6]

Yep, there you go again – As the father said, Vancouver Island trying to smear the guy!

As the father said, what a shyster outfit?

Justice Robert Johnston "found no error by the provincial court judge and dismissed the appeal by VIU and upheld him getting 75% of the $10,000. He also ordered that Kumar's $700 cost be paid to him as a lump sum by VIU."[7]

Good for you Avanish Kumar, you won one for "the little guy".

As the father asked, does anyone want to attend this college now?

Footnotes

1 - 2. *VIU loses lawsuit, appeal to foreign student*
The Daily News (Nanaimo) February 19, 2009

3. *Vancouver Island University – MBA*

4 - 2. *VIU loses lawsuit, appeal to foreign student*
The Daily News (Nanaimo) February 19, 2009

Chapter 12

Students suffer!

In another situation, the students again suffer.

As cited, "The faculty and administration at Vancouver Island University want to get back to the negotiating table as soon as possible after negotiations broke off Saturday, but both sides are far apart." [1]

"Meanwhile, students who gathered at the administration building on campus Monday expressed frustration with a seemingly endless strike that is interfering with their academic and personal lives." [2]

"We feel like pawns in a situation who don't have a voice in what's happening to us," said Matthew Clark, a hospitality management major. [3]

"We just get no sense of urgency from either side to come to a deal and end the strike." [4]

"International student Man-Ying Wong, who is in her last year of the tourism management program at VIU, said her visa expires soon after she was supposed to graduate in April, so if the semester is extended to make up for the lost time during the strike, she likely won't be able to finish her program." [5]

"Essentially, my education will be ruined and I'm beginning to think that I should have chosen another university to study in," she said. [5]

Bingo – as far as the father is concerned, that was the answer, this international student should have probably chosen another college – university to study at?

Continuing, this international student said "I paid $12,000 per year to study at VIU and now it appears that my education may be ruined. This strike is putting students like me through a lot of stress and that's not fair." [6]

According to the father, very apparent that the college – university administration and the faculty are more interested in protecting themselves, and don't give a darn about how it affects the students – including international students on limited study visas?

To prove the point, for example, "Patrick Barbosa, organizer of VIU's student union, said the strike has already wreaked havoc on some students' semesters. He said students who are studying dental hygiene, nursing and education, as well as some trades programs, have been severely affected by the strike."[7]

"For some students who had provincial exams or practicum deadlines, [the strike] actually cost them the semester," Barbosa said.[8]

Footnotes

1 - 6. *VIU, faculty in stalemate with no new talks planned*
Robert Barron, The Daily News
Published: Tuesday, March 22, 2011

7 - 8. *Faculty suing Vancouver Island University*
By: Erika Stark   Post Date: Thu, 07/04/2011 - 9:14am
Charlatan Publications Inc.

Chapter 13

Administration sued!

To show what a dog-eat-dog life it is at this college – university, as far as the father can see, this news story may say it all "Union hits VIU with lawsuit - Faculty association claims newspaper ads run by administration were defamatory."[1]

As reported, "the administration at Vancouver Island University has been slapped with a defamation lawsuit by the striking VIU Faculty Association."[2]

"The lawsuit is over advertisements placed in several mid-Island newspapers, including the Daily News, in which the university outlines its views on what the faculty is seeking to achieve in negotiations and VIU's position on the bargaining points."[3]

"The VIUFA alleges that the defendants either participated in, or approved of, an advertisement that, in the guise of providing the public with the 'truth' about bargaining at VIU, attempted to damage VIUFA's reputation and weaken its bargaining position in the ongoing labour dispute."[4]

As far as the father is concerned, if Patrick Ross is an example of the truth at this college – university [see Chapter 10], there is no such thing as "truth" coming out from this place?

As further reported, "VIUFA chief steward Dominique Roelants said the lawsuit includes allegations that, even after it was pointed out to VIU that their ad on March 16 contained 'false and defamatory' content, the administration republished the same content two days later."[5]

"They should stop lying about us and get back to the bargaining table," Roelants said.[6] That's right, said the father, lie and lie again – that seems typical of this college – university [see Chapters 3 and Chapter 8].

Footnotes

1 - 7. *Union hits VIU with lawsuit - Faculty association claims newspaper ads run by administration were defamatory* By Robert Barron, Nanaimo Daily News March 26, 2011

Chapter 14

College sued again!

As cited in Choromanski v. Malaspina University College, 2002 BCSC 771[1] maybe the manner of this college – university may be better understood?

As cited at para 1, "on November 10, 1998, the plaintiff, then a 42-year-old employee of the Department of Fisheries and Oceans, slipped and fell on the grounds of the defendant's Nanaimo campus while returning to his car following an evening class. This is an action for damages for the personal injuries sustained by the plaintiff as a result. The plaintiff alleges negligence and breach of the Occupiers Liability Act, R.S.B.C. 1996, c. 337. Both liability and damages are in issue."[2]

At para 2, "the plaintiff fell in the vicinity of a concrete sidewalk in the area of the defendant's campus known as the 'centre court'. He maintains that he slipped on a quantity of mud that had accumulated on the sidewalk."[3]

The issues appear at para 3, "there are two factual issues central to the question of liability. The primary issue is whether the plaintiff has proven on a balance of probabilities that he was walking on the sidewalk when he fell. Resolution of this issue involves, among other things, a determination of the admissibility of certain documentary evidence. A subsidiary issue is whether, and if so to what extent, there was mud on the sidewalk at the time the plaintiff fell. Because the state of the sidewalk is relevant to my conclusions on the issue of where and how the plaintiff fell, I will deal with it first. Before I do that, however, an appreciation of the undisputed circumstances surrounding the area of the accident is necessary."[4]

Background appears at paras 4 to 8, "the Nanaimo campus of Malaspina University College sits on a hillside. The physics building, in which the plaintiff attended his classes, is located at the western or upper end of the campus. The parking lot to which the plaintiff was returning at the time he fell is located on the eastern or lower end of the campus. After his class on the night in question, the plaintiff travelled from the physics building, down a series of stairs, and across the area known as the centre court. The centre court consists of a large sloping grass hill bounded by a series of concrete sidewalks. The theatre building is located east of the centre court; adjacent to that building, there are additional stairs which give access to one of several parking lots."[5]

"On November 10, 1998, the plaintiff drove to the defendant's campus, parked, and walked up the stairs to the centre court. He travelled through the centre court by way of the sidewalks. He testified that he arrived at the campus shortly after 6:30 p.m. as it was "getting dark". It had rained earlier that day and the ground was wet. The plaintiff testified that as he walked along the sidewalk, at the point he would later fall, he noticed mud on the sidewalk in two locations apparently the result of runoff from the grassy slope adjacent to the west side of the walkway."[6]

"The plaintiff said that as he was walking back to his car at approximately 8:30 p.m., he slipped on the mud in the area he had earlier noticed. His left leg slipped forward. He continued to slide forward until his foot hit the elevated edge of an adjacent concrete slab. His foot abruptly stopped, his leg buckled under him, and his ankle broke."[7]

"The plaintiff testified that he was in immediate and significant pain due to the injuries he sustained. He screamed and thereby attracted the attention of Dallas Friesen, a student who happened to be in the vicinity. Mr. Friesen could not see the plaintiff but followed the sound of his screams and found him lying on the sidewalk with his books scattered about. Mr. Friesen assisted the plaintiff to the nearest parking lot located just beyond the theatre building. En route he called the ambulance for assistance. The plaintiff was initially treated by a paramedic and then transported to the Nanaimo Regional Hospital where he received further medical attention."[8]

As the Honourable Mr. Justice G.M. Barrow noted at para 9 to 11, "the only evidence that the sidewalk at the location of the plaintiff's fall was covered in mud to the degree described by the plaintiff comes from the plaintiff himself. He testified he made his observations while en route to his class sometime after 6:30 p.m. Although it was "getting dark", the plaintiff testified that there was sufficient light to allow him to see mud on the sidewalk and the condition of the adjacent grassy slope. Indeed, he said he walked through the mud although he did not, at the time, "give it a thought".[9]

"The plaintiff testified that mud had accumulated in a similar way on two slabs of concrete in the vicinity of his fall. He described the mud by drawing on a photograph of the sidewalk contained in Exhibit 2 (Photograph 15). The mud formed a triangle with the base of the triangle running along the expansion joint from the western edge of each concrete slab (adjacent to the grassy hill) to a point approximately 2 1/2 feet towards the middle of the slab. The height of the triangle extended along the entire four-foot length of the western boundary of the concrete slab. The two slabs which were covered in mud in the manner described above were not contiguous to one another but were separated by a third concrete slab which was not, to any significant degree, covered in mud."[10]

"The photograph referred to above was taken in February 1999 by the plaintiff. In the photograph, it is apparent there is some discoloration of the surface of the concrete slabs. This appears to be due either to simple dampness or the presence of mud. The area actually affected, as revealed in the photograph, is but a very small portion of the area described by the plaintiff as having been covered in mud on the evening that he fell."[11]

Author's note, notice how the Honourable Mr. Justice G.M. Barrow is wording his comments, "The two slabs which were covered in mud in the manner described above were not contiguous to one another but were separated by a third concrete slab which was not, to any significant degree, covered in mud" and "it is apparent there is some discoloration of the surface of the concrete slabs. This appears to be due either to simple dampness or the presence of mud" and, once again, "the area actually affected, as revealed in the photograph, is but a very small portion of the area".

Why the slant?

Maybe it's due to, as cited at para 12, where the Honourable Mr. Justice G.M. Barrow reported "against the plaintiff's account of the state of the sidewalk, there is the evidence of Dallas Friesen and the evidence of four employees of the defendant. Mr. Friesen did not know the plaintiff prior to the evening of November 10, 1998. He was then a full-time student at Malaspina University College and had been since September 1997. He completed his studies in December 1998. In February 2001, he provided a statement to an insurance adjuster. In cross-examination, he adopted as true the following extract from that statement: I did not find the concrete path slippery that night. As a student at the College, I used that particular pathway multiple times every day and I do not recall if I ever saw any debris, mud or anything else on that concrete – I can't say for sure. I do recall that the concrete appeared to be older and well worn. I, personally, have never slipped on that pathway, nor did I find it to be particularly slippery in the time I went to college."[12]

Author's note, hmm, notice how the student didn't recall the plaintiff "screamed and thereby attracted the attention of Dallas Friesen, a student who happened to be in the vicinity. Mr. Friesen could not see the plaintiff but followed the sound of his screams and found him lying on the sidewalk with his books scattered about. Mr. Friesen assisted the plaintiff to the nearest parking lot located just beyond the theatre building. En route he called the ambulance for assistance."

Unless the plaintiff is in the habit of falling down, books strewn all over the place, and screaming for no apparent reason – why would the student forget this episode?

And, why would the student phone for an ambulance?

In any event, the Honourable Mr. Justice G.M. Barrow reported further at paras 13 to 17, "Mr. Manfield is the defendant's [the college – university] manager of environmental health at the Nanaimo campus. He has been employed at that campus since September 1996. He spoke with the plaintiff on November 12, 1998, some two days after the accident. Following that conversation, he testified that he went to the centre court area of the campus and examined the vicinity generally. Although he did not know the precise location of the plaintiff's accident at the time of his attendance, he testified that he had never seen mud accumulated on the sidewalk in question to the degree described by the plaintiff at any time during his employment with the defendant. He further testified that he would, in the course of his duties, walk along the centre court sidewalks at least once a week. He gave evidence that it was not uncommon to see the limited degree of mud as shown in Photographs 15 and 16 of Exhibit 2. He was of the view that the mud was washed on and off by the rainfalls."[13]

"Mr. Howe testified that he has worked for the defendant [the college – university] for 12 years as its head groundskeeper.

His duties, and those of the two full-time staff he supervises, include ensuring the campus grounds are safe. To that end, he walks extensively over the campus and, in particular, he walks the centre court area at least once a day, except on those relatively infrequent occasions when his other duties require him to be off campus. He testified that he has never seen the sidewalk in the area of the plaintiff's accident covered in mud to the extent described by the plaintiff. Indeed, he has never seen the sidewalk covered in mud to the extent that it required cleaning otherwise than in conjunction with the annual general campus cleanup. Mr. Howe walked the area on November 12th after learning of the plaintiff's accident and did not observe mud as described by the plaintiff. In fact, he did not observe anything which caused him to take any remedial steps in the area in question."[14]

"Stephen Schmidt is one of the two employees that make up the full-time members of Mr. Howe's grounds crew. He has worked at the defendant's [the college – university] campus for six years. He testified that safety is a constant concern in his job and that if he saw a hazard, he would, depending on its nature, either mark the area to warn others and then arrange to have it cleaned, or clean it up immediately. He said that he uses the centre court sidewalks at least once a week. He testified that he has never seen mud on the sidewalk to the extent described by the plaintiff. He said that if he had, he would regard it as a hazard and would clean it up. He said he has never had to clean mud from the sidewalk in the area of the plaintiff's accident, either on his own initiative or at the request of his supervisor or others."[15]

"Stephen Hughes is the other full-time groundskeeper employed by the defendant [the college – university]. He testified that he has worked at the defendant's Nanaimo campus in that capacity for ten years. Like Mr. Schmidt, he said that the safety of the students and other users of the campus grounds is always a concern of his. He looks for potential hazards, as well as remediating those that are brought to his attention by others. Mr. Hughes testified that he walks the centre court area of the campus approximately twice a week. He said that he has never seen mud on the sidewalk in the area of the plaintiff's fall to the extent described by the plaintiff. If he had, he would regard it as a hazard and clean it up. He said that he has never been directed to clean the area in question throughout his tenure as a groundskeeper."[16]

"All three of the groundskeepers employed by the defendant said that mud from time to time accumulates in the expansion joints and sometimes extends somewhat beyond the expansion joints, particularly on the uphill or western side of the sidewalk. The photographs taken by the plaintiff and admitted into evidence show some mud in the vicinity of the expansion joints. As noted, however, the area covered is but a small fraction of the area the plaintiff described as being present on the night he fell. Neither Mr. Hughes nor Mr. Schmidt regard the accumulation of mud to the degree actually shown in the photographs as uncommon and neither considered it a hazard."[17]

As the Honourable Mr. Justice G.M. Barrow concludes at para 18, "I recognize that the Mr. Hughes, Mr. Schmidt and Mr. Howe are all employees of the defendant [the college – university]. I also recognize that to some degree the diligence with which they discharged their responsibilities is called into question in this case. They gave their evidence in a balanced, careful and forthright manner. I accept their evidence without hestiation."[18]

Why not, said the father?

Just one establishment [the justice department] supporting another establishment [the college – university]?

After all, as the father said, according to these employees, the campus sidewalks are spotless – brushed, shovelled, sanded to perfection?

What a joke, he said.

The times his children attended the college – university, snow, ice, mud were quite common during inclement weather?

The father can't recall seeing any grounds-crew scouring the campus as described by the EMPLOYEES of the college – university as described in this particular case [see paras 13 to 18]?

Why not, it's only a "little guy" faculty member and we've seen how the college – university treats its faculty "they should stop lying about us and get back to the bargaining table," Roelants said [see the previous chapter, Chapter 15].

As also recorded at para 29, "Mr. Choromanski's lack of facility with the English language" [19] – ah, is that the rub, as the father stated, not only was the plaintiff a "little guy" faculty member – his English wasn't that hot – surely easy pickings for this college – university and the court hearing his case, as the father reasoned.

Sure enough, as the father thought, the Honourable Mr. Justice G.M. Barrow shoves it to the plaintiff one more time in para 19, "although no witness, other than the plaintiff, could say what the sidewalk was like on the evening of November 10th, it is odd that similar conditions were not observed by any witnesses on any other occasion during the balance of the month or at any other time for that matter."[20]

"I am not satisfied on a balance of probabilities that the sidewalk was covered in mud to the degree described by the plaintiff."[21]

And one more time at para 32, with the Honourable Mr. Justice G.M. Barrow stating "the plaintiff testified that he slipped on a substantial quantity of mud which he maintains had accumulated on one of the concrete slabs. He testified that he slid across a second slab which was not covered in mud and across a third slab which was covered in mud, until his forward progress was stopped by his foot coming into contact with the raised edge of a fourth concrete slab. I gather from his evidence that he has never been in doubt about the manner or place in which the accident occurred. I do not doubt that the plaintiff sincerely believes that the accident occurred as he now recalls it. I am not, however, satisfied on a balance of probabilities that it did."[22]

Footnotes

1 - 22. *Choromanski v. Malaspina University College*, 2002 BCSC 771

Chapter 15

A favourite scam by Human Rights – Continuing!

So called Human Rights Commissions or Tribunals will do everything in their power to 'abridge' the rights of the "little guy" in order to protect government departments, institutions, companies, corporations using the feeblest of excuses.

Yep, what a College, the father tries to protect his children from a lying professor and he is banned from campus?

Seems quiet typical behaviour of Malaspina University College?

What's most important in this process, is that it's a typical scam by Human Rights Departments in Canada to use the "buzz word", even if the discrimination has life-long consequences, unless the discrimination is repeated, and repeated, and repeated [i.e., "continuing"] the lone individual making the complaint is sheer out of luck!

As cited at paragraph 24 of the instant complaint before the British Columbia Human Rights Tribunal, Lindsay M. Lyster, Tribunal Member reporting:

That there must be an alleged contravention in order for there to be a continuing contravention is apparent on the face of s. 22(2). In what remains the leading decision on continuing contraventions, Lynch, supra, the British Columbia Supreme Court adopted, at para. 35, the following statement from the Manitoba Court of Appeal's decision in Re The Queen in Right of Manitoba and Manitoba Human Rights Commission et al. reflex, (1984), 2 D.L.R. (4th) 759:

To be a "continuing contravention", there must be a succession or repetition of separate acts of discrimination of the same character. There must be present acts of discrimination which could be considered as separate contraventions of the Act, and not merely one act of discrimination which may have continuing effects of consequences. (emphasis added)

In other words, the "little guy" is screwed every time!

Unless the "little guy" can prove a continuing repetition of the discrimination, they are screwed – even if the initial discrimination has a life-long effect?

Incredibly, the British Columbia Human Rights Tribunal member Lindsay M. Lyster makes reference at paragraph 21 to looking at Dove v. Greater Vancouver Regional District (No. 3), 2006 BCHRT 374 to help determine "what constitutes a continuing contravention of the Code".

However, in examining Dove v. Greater Vancouver Regional District (No. 3), 2006 BCHRT 374 it is very clear, as cited at paragraph 21 of that case, despite suffering 20 years of discrimination "the burden is on the complainant to establish that his complaint … [is] sufficient to establish a continuing contravention."

In other words, the British Columbia Human Rights Tribunal has no intention of investigating discrimination by a lone individual, that "little guy" has to do their job for them?

How many "little guys" can do that?

Who was the deciding member from the British Columbia Human Rights Tribunal in the Dove v. Greater Vancouver Regional District (No. 3), 2006 BCHRT 374 case?

Why, none other than Lindsay M. Lyster?

How ironic?

In fact in Dove v. Greater Vancouver Regional District (No. 3), 2006 BCHRT 374, Lindsay M. Lyster really put the screws to Mr. Dove when, as cited at paragraph 22 of that case, although "Mr. Dove added allegations of events since February 2006, and added the ground of mental disability" Lindsay M. Lyster agreed "with the respondents that the contents of the amended complaint are irrelevant to the present application, which deals solely with the original complaint."

So, in other words, when Mr. Dove tried to show a continuing discrimination, Lindsay M. Lyster kept him to the "original complaint", citing "the apparent intermixing of information relevant to the original and amended complaint is unfortunate, as I have no way of knowing which aspects of the alleged profiling and other acts of discrimination relate to the original!

Chapter 16

A favourite scam by Human Rights - Public Interest!

So called Human Rights Commissions or Tribunals will do everything in their power to 'abridge' the rights of the "little guy" in order to protect government departments, institutions, companies, corporations using the feeblest of excuses.

Yep, what a College, the father tries to protect his children from a lying professor and he is banned from campus?

Seems quiet typical behaviour of Malaspina University College?

What's most important in this process is another typical scam by Human Rights Departments in Canada to use the "buzz word" in the public interest – again the lone individual making the complaint is sheer out of luck!

Obviously the human rights violations suffered by the lone individual may well not be of interest to the general public – but it gives the so called Human Rights Commissions or Tribunals in Canada to dismiss any such "lone individual" complaint.

As cited at paragraph 35 of the instant complaint before the British Columbia Human Rights Tribunal, Lindsay M. Lyster, Tribunal Member refers to Gray v. Northwest Community College and others, 2009 BCHRT 26 in limiting the "lone individual" complaint.

In looking at Gray v. Northwest Community College and others, 2009 BCHRT 26, although it cites at para 13 that it is important to ensure "that vulnerable persons have access to the Tribunal" this case too used the "not in the public interest" buzz word to dismiss the complaint of Ms. Gray at para 20 "I therefore conclude that it would not be in the public interest to accept the complaint for filing."

Who was the deciding member from the British Columbia Human Rights Tribunal in the Gray v. Northwest Community College and others, 2009 BCHRT 26 case?

Why, again, none other than Lindsay M. Lyster?

How ironic?

Do you see a pattern here?

Screw with the "little guy" again?

In that case [Gray v. Northwest Community College and others, 2009 BCHRT 26], Ms. Gray.

In the instant case, the father who tries to protect his children from a lying professor and he is banned from campus?

Notice in the instant case, there is absolutely no reference to the initial reason for the father's involvement – the lying professor, Helen Brown?

Does this explain the miserable mistreatment of this young student by Malaspina University-College (a.k.a. Vancouver Island university)?

Chapter 17

A favorite scam of Human Rights – Use Words of Discriminator!

So called Human Rights Commissions or Tribunals will do everything in their power to 'abridge' the rights of the "little guy" in order to protect government departments, institutions, companies, corporations using the feeblest of excuses.

Yep, what a College, the father tries to protect his children from a lying professor and he is banned from campus?

Seems quiet typical behaviour of Malaspina University College?

What's most important in this process is another typical scam by Human Rights Departments in Canada to use the use words of discriminator – and none from the "little guy" - again the lone individual making the complaint is sheer out of luck [see Appendix 11]!

In the instant case, British Columbia Human Rights Tribunal member Lindsay M. Lyster made absolutely no reference to the initial reason for the father's involvement – the lying professor, Helen Brown?

Lindsay M. Lyster, however, did refer to the respondent's [the college – university] assertions "In general terms, the respondents say that [the father] was confrontational, and his conduct unacceptable."

In response, the father "characterizes all such assertions on the respondents' part as 'outright lies'."

Good for the father!

Could this further explain the fact that in the instant case British Columbia Human Rights Tribunal member Lindsay M. Lyster made absolutely no reference to the initial reason for the father's involvement – the lying professor, Helen Brown?

Again, in the realm of possibility, sure it does?

Chapter 18

A favorite scam of Human Rights – Ignore the Words of Person Being Discriminated!

So called Human Rights Commissions or Tribunals will do everything in their power to 'abridge' the rights of the "little guy" in order to protect government departments, institutions, companies, corporations using the feeblest of excuses.

In the previous chapter, it was mentioned that British Columbia Human Rights Tribunal member Lindsay M. Lyster made absolutely no reference to the initial reason for the father's involvement – the lying professor, Helen Brown?

Lindsay M. Lyster, however, did refer to the respondent's [the college – university] assertions "In general terms, the respondents say that [the father] was confrontational, and his conduct unacceptable."

In response, the father "characterizes all such assertions on the respondents' part as 'outright lies'."

In typical fashion of Human Rights in Canada, British Columbia Human Rights Tribunal member Lindsay M. Lyster then used her decision in the instant case to kybosh another lone individual.

Specifically, in Fraser v. College of New Caledonia and others, 2009 BCHRT 432[1], where the lone complainant Shelley Fraser pitted herself against College of New Caledonia, Patricia Noble, Sandra Ollech, Kerry Hart, Georgina Jones, Lynn Jacques, Wendy King (Jobs), Karen Lange, Ebony Bilawka, Carrie De Palma, Heather Mohr, John Bowman, Kim Saliken, Susan Toyata, Gregory Ames, Leslie Battersby, Patricia Covington, Margit Strobl and Carole Whitmer.

Wow, can you see where this is going before you even read British Columbia Human Rights Tribunal member Lindsay M. Lyster's decision in Ms. Shelley Fraser case?

In this case too, just like the father, represented herself.

At para 1, Lindsay M. Lyster cites "Shelley Fraser filed a complaint alleging that she was discriminated against on the basis of race and ancestry in the course of her studies in the Dental Hygienist Program (the

"Program") at the College of New Caledonia (the "College"), contrary to s. 8 of the Human Rights Code. Ms. Fraser is Métis."

At para 4, Lindsay M. Lyster reports the quandary "I decide whether the complaint alleges a contravention of the Code, and to the extent it does, whether it was filed in time. To the extent the complaint alleges a contravention of the Code, but does so out of time, I decide whether to exercise my discretion to accept it."

Ah, yes, another favourite – the time line – if registered "in time".

As cited in Chartier v. School District No. 62, 2003 BCHRT 39 at para 9, under Bill 64 which came into effect 31 March, 2003 "the time for filing a human rights complaint was reduced from one year to six months from the date of the alleged contravention."

Why not, British Columbia, make it even more difficult for the person complaining about human rights violations?

After all, it does take some time to find a lawyer in Canada to take your case.[2]

As cited at para 5, British Columbia Human Rights Tribunal member Lindsay M. Lyster mentions her decision, "I have decided not to accept the complaint for filing."

What was Ms. Fraser's complaint?

Although Lindsay M. Lyster found "Ms. Fraser's complaint is lengthy and difficult to summarize" [para 6], Lyster did mention the following incidents:

At para 7, "The first incident alleged is the only one which includes any explicit reference to Ms. Fraser's race or ancestry. Ms. Fraser alleges that, sometime within the first two weeks of September 2006, the students in the Program were required to pay a deposit for the rental of an instrument kit. There was a list at the instructor's station with students' names on it indicating whether they had paid. Ms. Fraser alleges that, when she went to see if the list showed her as being paid, four instructors (all named as respondents to the complaint) were looking at the list and talking. She alleges that one of the instructors said, in a sarcastic context, No she does not need to pay because the whole program is being funded for her by the Métis''."

As further cited in text of this particular case, "Ms. Noble is alleged to have made the comment quoted above at paragraph 7 about funding for

Ms. Fraser. In addition, she is alleged to have made a negative comment about Ms. Fraser's hair in the context of an evaluation on professional appearance, to have refused to tell Ms. Fraser where certain forms were kept, to have spoken to Ms. Fraser in a humiliating and threatening way while demonstrating a technique, and to have told other students about a sensitive family matter of Ms. Fraser's."

At para 8, Ms. Fraser reasoned, "The instructors obviously did not approve of me being funded by the Métis BC Nation and were made aware of my aboriginal ancestry. I believe that after this comment was made that I was racially discriminated against. I believe that this was a form of subtle and subversive discrimination because I was excessively monitored and documented, disproportionately blamed for incidents and accused of being confrontational by staff and faculty members when I was asked to provide my opinion or rationale for something, and penalized for not getting along with others when the other faculty members or staff members were engaged in racialized behaviour against me. When I would seek assistance from faculty and followed through with their recommendations I was constantly reprimanded for it and accused of being unsafe. I was continually treated and graded differently than the other students that did not have aboriginal ancestry...."

Those incidents within the limited six months period, as noted in text included:

October 7, 2008 – Ms. Lange is alleged to have assigned Ms. Fraser an unsatisfactory grade, which Ms. Fraser alleges to have been "excessive and unfair".

October 23, 2008 – Ms. Fraser had a mandatory "teaching time" with Ms. Lange, during which Ms. Lange allegedly reprimanded her in front of the patient, and was rude to her. Ms. Fraser alleges that this was "unprofessional and harassing behaviour by faculty and [that she was] reprimanded for following instruction, false, misleading and excessive documentation."

November 6, 2008 – Ms. Strobl is alleged to have told Ms. Fraser her instruments were not sharp enough, resulting in her failing a "sharpness check". Ms. Fraser goes on to refer to the allegations, already recounted above, about Ms. Bilawka's allegedly inconsistent evaluation of the sharpness of her instruments. In relation to these incidents, Ms. Fraser alleges that "it appeared that anything I signed up for I would receive an unsatisfactory grade for because the instructors did not want me to graduate". She characterizes this as "unusual and suspicious behaviour from faculty, unfair grading".

November 13, 2008 – Ms. Strobl observed Ms. Fraser with the patient Ms. Bilawka had observed her with on the previous day. Ms. Fraser alleges that Ms. Strobl assigned her an unsatisfactory grade, and that "it was obvious to me that any performance evaluation I attempted I would fail because the instructors had once against collaborated to fail me". She alleges that this was "false documentation, unfair grading. I was being graded for causing tissue trauma when there wasn't any. Suspicious and unusual behaviour. Differential treatment than non aboriginal students."

October 28, 2008 – Ms. King observed Ms. Fraser with a patient. Ms. Fraser alleges that, in the course of doing so, Ms. King became very upset and yelled at her, and wrote on her daily progress form that she found Ms. Fraser's recollection of specific information suspicious. According to Ms. Fraser, Ms. King asked her if she could swear on a stack of bibles about her recollection of the patient's health history. Ms. Fraser also alleges that, during this observation, Ms. King sharpened Ms. Fraser's instrument on a wall and then gave the contaminated instrument back to her to use on her patient. Ms. Fraser alleges that Ms. King was rude and abused her authority to put her in her place. Ms. Fraser characterizes this as "harassing, disrespectful and threatening behaviour, as well as unusual decisions by a senior faculty member".

December 1, 2008 – Ms. Fraser met with her counsellor about applying to other colleges. Ms. Fraser alleges that her counsellor told her she had received telephone calls from Ms. King and Ms. Covington asking about her plans. She asked her counsellor if she thought her instructors would get involved and contact other colleges, and her counsellor told her it would be better to be on the safe side and not let her instructors know. Ms. Fraser alleges this "was a violation of my personal information and it was illegal."

October 16, 2008 – Ms. Mohr is alleged to have reprimanded Ms. Fraser for having a needle off of the syringe without a cartridge penetrating cover on it. Ms. Fraser alleges that she e-mailed Ms. Mohr about this incident and explained her conduct. Ms. Fraser alleges that this was "excessive and false documentation [and] unfair grading. Assignment of unsatisfactory grades on information not taught in the program. Differential treatment from non aboriginal students."

November 13, 2008 – Ms. Mohr observed Ms. Fraser with a patient, and is alleged to have written many negative comments about her. Ms. Mohr is alleged to have spoken with another faculty member, after which she assigned Ms. Fraser an unsatisfactory grade. Ms. Fraser alleges that Ms. Mohr engaged in this behaviour "to keep excessive negative documentation on me". She characterizes it as "harassing and suspicious behaviour".

October 20, 2008 - Ms. Fraser alleges that Ms. Battersby gave her an unsatisfactory grade because of where she found one of her patient charts, which Ms. Fraser alleges to have been "differential treatment than non aboriginal students and grading that was different from customary standards."

October 21, 2008 – Ms. Fraser alleges that Ms. Battersby assigned her an unsatisfactory grade for nicking a patient's tissues, despite other instructors saying that bleeding was normal in a patient of this kind. Ms. Fraser also repeats the allegation that another student cut this patient without receiving an unsatisfactory grade, and alleges that this was "different grading than non aboriginal students".

October 23, 2008 – Ms. Fraser alleges that Ms. Battersby wrote that she needed to slow down and be more careful flossing or she would cause trauma, but that she had never caused trauma flossing. She characterizes this as "false documentation and harassing behaviour."

November 12, 2008 – Ms. Fraser alleges that Ms. Battersby observed her with a patient, and assigned her an unsatisfactory grade for not immediately covering the cartridge penetrating end of a needle. She alleges that Ms. Battersby wrote on her form with her latex gloves on, which if she had done would have resulted in an unsatisfactory grade. In the course of treating this same patient, the patient complained of soreness, which Ms. Battersby wrote was the result of Ms. Fraser giving an injection incorrectly. Ms. Fraser says that this was "misleading and fabricated information. Harassing and disrespectful behaviour along with excessive and false documentation."

November 5, 2008 – Ms. Fraser alleges that Ms. Ollech told her she wanted to have a personal meeting with her. They met, and Ms. Ollech advised Ms. Fraser that she was not to discuss the Committee's recommendations with the students on that Committee any further, and should pose any questions she might have to her. Ms. Fraser further alleges that Ms. Ollech told her that her request to have a third party present during evaluative meetings had been denied, which she found "suspicious and harassing".

Author's note, the father said this is quite typical behaviour of liars – they do not want third parties involved – liars want no witnesses to their lies!

November 14, 2008 - Ms. Fraser repeats her allegations about the meeting with Ms. Ollech, Ms. Bilawka, Ms. King and her counsellor. Ms. Fraser alleges that Ms. Ollech made no comments during the meeting. As stated elsewhere, Ms. Fraser says that it was at this point that she decided she could not continue in the Program, and that she asked about what information they would provide to other colleges to which she applied. She alleges that they told her they could only provide information she consented to, and that Ms. Ollech said she was brave for asking for the meeting. At the end of the meeting, Ms. Fraser alleges that she told Ms. Ollech she could not sign the Academic Probation and Learning Contract because it was full of discrepancies, and a violation of her freedom of speech.

This summary does not include all actions prior to the six-month time limit and those partly prior to six-month time limit.

However, the reader may see the gist of Ms. Fraser's complaint?

Seems reasonable, doesn't it?

Well, let's see how British Columbia Human Rights Tribunal member Lindsay M. Lyster decides in Ms. Shelley Fraser case?

In spite of stating at para 4 that she has discretion to accept a complaint out of time ["To the extent the complaint alleges a contravention of the Code, but does so out of time, I decide whether to exercise my discretion to accept it"], does British Columbia Human Rights Tribunal member Lindsay M. Lyster do so in fairness to Ms. Fraser?

Under IV analysis, it is cited at para 13, "Ms. Fraser submits that her complaint is timely, because it constitutes a timely continuing contravention of the Code pursuant to s. 22(2), and should be accepted on that basis. In the alternative, she submits that the Tribunal should exercise its discretion to accept any late-filed parts of her complaint."

In an effort to ignore the words of person being discriminated, the British Columbia Human Rights Tribunal has implemented a nice little trick as a buffer to whether it accepts a complaint or not.

That buffer, a "screening" process.

As cited at para 17, Tribunal member Lindsay M. Lyster states "Prior to accepting complaints for filing, the Tribunal, in accordance with its Rules of Practice and Procedure, 'screens' complaints to ensure, inter alia, that they appear to be within the Tribunal's jurisdiction, and to allege a timely contravention of the Code. The current decision arises within the context of that screening process, as the complaint has, to date, only been accepted for the limited purposes of screening it."

In para 20, Tribunal member Lindsay M. Lyster postulates "In the present case, there are some allegations within the six-month time limit, in addition to many more allegations prior to that date. The respondents' submissions raise two questions: are any of the allegations, whether prior to or after the six-month time limit, allegations of a contravention of the Code? And if they are, are they continuing in nature so as to make the earlier allegations timely?"

Ms. Fraser counters at para 21, "Ms. Fraser responds to these questions, submitting: first, that each allegation in her complaint is an allegation of a contravention of the Code; and second, that they are continuing in nature, so as to make the earlier allegations, and the complaint as a whole, timely."

Tribunal member Lindsay M. Lyster continues at para 22 with "In the circumstances of this complaint, I find it appropriate to consider first whether any part of the complaint, whether filed before or after the six-month time limit, alleges an arguable contravention of the Code ... Fair to Ms. Fraser, because given the extensive and detailed nature of her complaint, in which she has set out every possible fact upon which her complaint could be based, it is fair to subject her complaint to an inquiry about whether it alleges an arguable contravention of the Code ... It is also fair to the respondents, especially the 18 individual instructors and administrators, who should not have the complaint accepted against them unless, at a minimum, it contains allegations of fact which, if proven, could establish discrimination on their part."

So, if British Columbia Human Rights Tribunal member Lindsay M. Lyster acting as judge, jury and executioner, decides that none of the "discriminatory" behaviour against Ms. Fraser constitutes a human rights violation [as far as Lindsay M. Lyster is concerned] that's it for Ms. Fraser and her complaint – sayonara?

At para 25, Lindsay M. Lyster states "Here, where the grounds of race and ancestry are relied upon, Ms. Fraser must allege facts that, if proven, could establish that she has in some way been adversely affected by reason of, or in relation to, being Métis. It is not enough for her to say that she is Métis and has been treated unfairly. There must be some arguable connection or nexus between the two."

At para 26, it is cited "The respondents submit that Ms. Fraser's complaint does not fulfil this requirement. In this connection, they note that the only allegation that even refers to Ms. Fraser's race and ancestry is the alleged remark in September 2006 about her being funded by the Métis Nation. They submit that this alleged remark is entirely benign, and cannot be construed as an even arguable contravention of the Code. The respondents further submit that all of Ms. Fraser's remaining allegations, whether within the six-month time limit or not, lack any basis upon which one could reasonably infer any connection between the adverse treatment she alleges and the fact that she is Métis."

At para 27, "In response, Ms. Fraser acknowledges that the September 2006 remark about her funding for the Program would not alone have been sufficient to prove discrimination. She submits, however, that that remark, together with the ensuing events, establishes a pattern of subtle and subversive discrimination. In this connection, she relies on Tribunal case law which recognizes that racial discrimination is often subtle, and that findings of discrimination require that inferences be drawn from the treatment of the complainant as compared to others: see, for example, Poon v. Downes and ACL Services, 2006 BCHRT 353, paras. 9 - 10."

Continuing with, at para 28 "Ms. Fraser further notes that she has documented from one to ten separate acts of discrimination in every month in which she was in the Program, with the exception only of vacation and break periods."

What does British Columbia Human Rights Tribunal member Lindsay M. Lyster conclude?

At paras 29 to 31, Lindsay M. Lyster states:

[29] I accept that racism today is less likely to be overt and more likely to be subtle. This is probably especially likely to be true in the comparatively sophisticated context of post-secondary educational institutions. I also accept that findings of discrimination in such circumstances are likely to be made on the basis of inferences from facts, and from examining the treatment of the complainant as compared to the others.

[30] Nonetheless, while racism may be subtle, the discrimination alleged to have been caused by it must be discernable. In other words, the allegations made must be capable of establishing the reasonable inference that the adverse treatment alleged was related to race and ancestry.

[31] Applying these principles to this case, I conclude that Ms. Fraser has failed to allege facts from which it could reasonably be inferred that she was discriminated against on the basis of her race or ancestry.

With Lindsay M. Lyster concluding at para 35, "I conclude that the complaint fails to allege an arguable contravention of the Code, whether timely or not. I decline to accept it on that basis."

Oh, my God?

British Columbia Human Rights Tribunal member Lindsay M. Lyster has done it – sayonara Ms. Fraser and your [legitimate] complaint?

The only problem with British Columbia Human Rights Tribunal member Lindsay M. Lyster's conclusion, however, is that she has selectively cited cases that might support her decision?

Such as Poon v. Downes and ACL Services, 2006 BCHRT 353, where "Mr. Poon's allegations are not of overt racist comments or actions." [3]

Interestingly, as cited elsewhere, "the majority of Race cases that go before the Tribunal result in a finding that there was no discrimination." [4]

However, it appears that Lindsay M. Lyster ignored other citations?

For example, in Radek v. Henderson Development (Canada) and Securiguard Services (No. 3), 2005 BCHRT 302 it is stated:

a) The prohibited ground or grounds of discrimination need not be the sole or the major factor leading to the discriminatory conduct; it is sufficient if they are a factor;
b) There is no need to establish an intention or motivation to discriminate; the focus of the inquiry is on the effect of the respondent's actions on the complainant;
c) The prohibited ground or grounds need not be the cause of the respondent's discriminatory conduct; it is sufficient if they are a factor or operative element;
d) There need be no direct evidence of discrimination; discrimination will more often be proven by circumstantial evidence and inference. [5]

It appears that Lindsay M. Lyster ignored the key phrase here, "There is no need to establish an intention or motivation to discriminate; the focus of the inquiry is on the effect of the respondent's actions on the complainant." [6]

Maybe the discrimination of Ms. Fraser wasn't overt enough for British Columbia Human Rights Tribunal member Lindsay M. Lyster?

Maybe had Ms. Fraser suffered as that in Small Legs v. Dhillon, 2008 BCHRT 104 [7] that would have met Lindsay M. Lyster's cut-off point?

In Small Legs v. Dhillon, 2008 BCHRT, cited elsewhere, "In that case the Complainant confronted the respondent, her employer, about being paid a minimum wage. It was alleged that the respondent started screaming at the complainant, calling her a "stupid f***ing Indian", and told her to pack her equipment (brushes, scissors and shears) and get the "hell out of the salon" where she worked."[8]

In that case, "The Tribunal Member found that there had been a breach of the Human Rights Code and awarded $2,000 for injury to dignity." [9]

One last detail about Ms. Fraser's case, it is very interesting to note this statement at para 11:

December 1, 2008 – Ms. Fraser met with her counsellor about applying to other colleges. Ms. Fraser alleges that her counsellor told her she had received telephone calls from Ms. King and Ms. Covington asking about her plans. She asked her counsellor if she thought her instructors would get involved and contact other colleges, and her counsellor told her it would be better to be on the safe side and not let her instructors know. Ms. Fraser alleges this "was a violation of my personal information and it was illegal."[11]

Interesting – did these instructors conspire to try to kybosh Ms. Fraser with other colleges?

Makes one of British Columbia Human Rights Tribunal member Lindsay M. Lyster's concluding comments at para 49 somewhat superfluous[12], "Ms. Fraser's complaint is speculative in nature. She asks the Tribunal to conclude that 19 respondents, over a period of more than two years, engaged in a concerted effort to harass her, grade her unfairly, monitor and document her, all the apparent object of forcing her out of the Program because her funding came from the Métis Nation. No reason is advanced as to why the 19 named respondents would have done so. Ms. Fraser's complaint rests upon an inherently implausible premise, which the facts alleged by her do not tend to substantiate."[13]

Is the proof in how senseless Lindsay M. Lyster's comment is quite simply revealed, again in the incident cited above: *December 1, 2008 – Ms. Fraser met with her counsellor about applying to other colleges. Ms. Fraser alleges that her counsellor told her she had received telephone calls from Ms. King and Ms. Covington asking about her plans. She asked her counsellor if she thought her instructors would get involved and contact other colleges, and her counsellor told her it would be better to be on the safe side and not let her instructors know. Ms. Fraser alleges this "was a violation of my personal information and it was illegal."*[11]

Again, why did these instructors [Ms. King and Ms. Covington] want to know Ms. Fraser's plans?

Better yet, why didn't British Columbia Human Rights Tribunal member Lindsay M. Lyster want to know?

Footnotes

1 - 2. *Fraser v. College of New Caledonia and others, 2009 BCHRT 432*

3 – 9. News from the B.C. Human Rights Coalition, Volume 9.2, April 2009: March 21 – International Day for the Elimination of Racial Discrimination

10 - 11. *Fraser v. College of New Caledonia and others, 2009 BCHRT 432*

12. So there no misunderstanding of how the author has used this term: superfluous - serving no useful purpose; "a pointless remark"; senseless

13. *Fraser v. College of New Caledonia and others, 2009 BCHRT 432*

Chapter 19

Notice no mention of lying professor!

Notice how there is absolutely no mention by Lindsay M. Lyster, Tribunal Member about the initial reason this father was involved with Malaspina University College (a.k.a. Vancouver Island University).

Remember the reason – remember the lying professor, Helen Brown.

As cited in Chapter 3 of this book, it all started in November, 2005 when Malaspina University College "professor" Helen Brown in the History Department wrote on one of this young fellow's papers "an important part of preparing for the final exam is attending class. You have missed 10 of 19 classes in addition to arriving 50 minutes late for another" [see Appendix 1].

Well, for one, the boy's father knew full-well that this was an outright lie because he was retired and drove his son to Malaspina University College.

The boy's father knew full-well that his son had not missed 10 of 19 classes and he was never 50 minutes late for a class.

When this a fine young student confronted this liar of a professor on 10th November, this Malaspina University College "professor" Helen Brown retracted her "estimate" downward to something more approaching the truth [see Appendix 2a & 2b]

This interaction is referred to in a letter dated 24th November, 2005 written by the boy's father to the Dean of Arts and Humanities, Steven M. Lane, at this Malaspina University College about this liar of a "professor". The letter speaks for itself, and appears in Appendix 2a and 2b.

What did this liar of a "professor" do in a vindictive reaction to the father's letter written 24th November, 2005 complaining about "professor" Helen Brown initial lie – she repeated her lie on the boy's final written assignment for her History 476 class presented to her on 24th November and returned to the boy later [see Appendix 3].

As appearing in Appendix 3, this liar of a professor as the father calls her, again stated "You were absent for many classes and that impacts on your participation grade" [see Appendix 3].

Quite typical of any government department trying to protect liars, try to smear the person putting in the complaint?

Such was the case with Lindsay M. Lyster, Tribunal Member of the British Columbia Human Rights Tribunal?

Leave the "juicy bits" out about the lying professor?

Also, note, this father represented himself at the Tribunal:

Tribunal Member: Lindsay M. Lyster

On his own behalf: The father

Counsel for the Respondents: D. Mark Gyton

As mentioned, so called Human Rights Commissions or Tribunals will do everything in their power to 'abridge' the rights of the "little guy" in order to protect government departments, institutions, companies, corporations using the feeblest of excuses.

Chapter 20

The lying professor goes after daughter too!

The proof is in the pudding, not only did the lying professor try to get the father's son with lies, it all started in November, 2005 when Malaspina University College "professor" Helen Brown in the History Department wrote on one of this young fellow's papers "an important part of preparing for the final exam is attending class. You have missed 10 of 19 classes in addition to arriving 50 minutes late for another" [see Appendix 1].

As also mentioned, when this a fine young student confronted this liar of a professor on 10th November, this Malaspina University College "professor" Helen Brown retracted her "estimate" downward to something more approaching the truth [see Appendix 2a & 2b]

This interaction is referred to in a letter dated 24th November, 2005 written by the boy's father to the Dean of Arts and Humanities, Steven M. Lane, at this Malaspina University College about this liar of a "professor". The letter speaks for itself, and appears in Appendix 2a and 2b.

What did this liar of a "professor" do in a vindictive reaction to the father's letter written 24th November, 2005 complaining about "professor" Helen Brown initial lie – she repeated her lie on the boy's final written assignment for her History 476 class presented to her on 24th November and returned to the boy later [see Appendix 3].

As appearing in Appendix 3, this liar of a professor, again stated "You were absent for many classes and that impacts on your participation grade" [see Appendix 3].

She also tried the same lie on his daughter. As appearing in Appendix 18, this "lying bag of crap" as the father likes to call her, pulled the same crap with his daughter.

The daughter's father knew full-well that his daughter had not missed many classes as this professor Helen Brown commented [see Appendix 12].

Chapter 21

Letter of Apology by British Columbia Human Rights Tribunal Lindsay M. Lyster!

An open letter to Terry Mallenby,
Re: Mallenby v. Malaspina University College and others, 2009 BCHRT 208:

Terry Mallenby, BA, BSW, MA
former federal peace officer
former Classification Officer BC Maximum Security Penitentiary
former Classification Officer BC Medium Security Mountain Prison
former Probation Officer NFLD Social Services Department*
former Facility Operations Manager Whitbourne Youth Secure Custody

Dear Mr. Mallenby,

You are absolutely right.

I purposefully ignored that you were only protecting your children from the Professor who lied.

My position as British Columbia Human Rights Tribunal chief was to protect the University at any cost.

And that included ignoring the fact that some of the officials at the University lied in their testimony.

It also included ignoring the reason that you made the complaint in the first place, the fact that you were only protecting your children from a Professor who lied!

Signed,

Lindsay M. Lyster
British Columbia Human Rights Tribunal

APPENDICES

The case of the lying professor and the college that protected her?

<u>Appendix 1</u>

regards economical success. As seen in Tuttle and Raymond's article, if the government and childhood theorists are presented with a ~~oo problent~~ chance to make a profit off of children

an important part of preparing for the final exam is attending class. You have missed 10 of 19 classes in addition to arriving 30 minutes late for another.

you have done a good job with connections a situating the Dionne's in terms of the course literature

consider also what Raymond's article tells us about the nature of the field - i.e. history of childhood as a form of enquiry

Appendix 2a

24th November, 2005

Steven M. Lane, Dean   "Hand Delivered"
Faculty of Arts & Humanities
Malaspina University-College
Nanaimo, B.C.
CANADA V9R 5S5

Dear Mr. Lane,

I am under the impression that the field of History has, as one of its main tenents, a desire for accuracy.

In fact, the History Department's web page(s) seem to indicate the same:
"we provide training in logical thought and the evaluation of evidence, along with training in historical methods and research techniques"
http://www.mala.bc.ca/history/Content/why.htm
"The integrity and quality of our programme is important to us and our instructors are committed to the craft of teaching"
http://www.mala.bc.ca/history/Content/guidelin.htm

I thus find it very disturbing that one History Professor, Helen Brown, has sent a student, my son _____, a note clearly indicating, according to Dr. Brown, that he has missed over ½ the classes in her History course 476; specifically, supposedly 10 out of 19 classes [see attached copy of her note].

However, when _____ confronted Professor Brown on 10th November, 2005 about this statement, Professor Brown retracted her "estimate" downward to something more approaching the truth.

_____ followed this meeting with a hand delivered letter dated 10th November, 2005 with a copy to yourself.

In this letter, _____ clearly specifies that the missed classes due to illness was more like 5-6-7, the exact number unverifiable, as Dr. Brown did not refer to any written record of attendance during his meeting with Dr. Brown.

Appendix 2b

Since that date and the writing of this letter, Dr. Brown has not indicated in "any way shape or form" that Jeremy's letter contained any inaccuracies.

Thus, I would like to know what kind of negative impact Dr. Brown's inaccurate statement will have on Jeremy's efforts in her course.

Obviously, if she has the impression that he has skipped over half the classes, this may well have a negative impact on his marks; it's known as the "Halo Effect".

In fact, Dr. Brown saw   during his illness because he "had gotten out of his sick-bed" to write the mid-term [that's how devoted he is to his course work] but, on seeing   , Dr. Brown suggested that he return home.

At no time did Dr. Brown indicate that   's standing was in jeopardy; that is, not until   received this note from Dr. Brown that he had supposedly missed over ½ the classes for her course!

In closing, I find it most inappropriate for a University Professor to write a note to a student that is apparently not based on fact or evidence?

It surely doesn't show much respect for the recipient and, as my children expend a lot of effort on everything they do, especially their course work, I would like to know what assurances can you offer to ensure that both my children are not negatively impacted by this inaccurate statement by Dr. Brown.

I can clearly use the term "inaccurate" in my letter to you because, as I am retired, I drive both my children to the University and I know full-well that neither of my children have missed over ½ the classes for Dr. Brown's course!

I look forward to an early reply.

Sincerely,

Appendix 3

FINAL RESEARCH PAPER

Because of their Tragic Nature,
the Similarity of Childhood War Memories
Gives an Accurate Glimpse into that Period of History

Submitted To:
Dr. Helen Brown
History 476: Modern Childhood

Date Due/Submitted:
24 November, 2005

Appendix 4

Helen Brown

From: @aol.com
Sent: Monday, October 17, 2005 10:35 PM
To: Helen Brown
Subject: sick

Dear Dr. Brown,

If it doesn't rain .. it pours!

It is 10:30 p.m. Monday night and   is stuck in the bathroom throwing-up, with some sort of flu.

He has been under the weather for a few days now and we thought he was on the mend, but obviously not yet.

I will be driving   -   to campus tomorrow for the Midterm.

Hopefully,   will be in some sort of shape to sit the Midterm.

However, if   is just too sick to sit in class doing the Midterm, is there any way that I can pick up the
Midterm for   , he does it at home [with supervision], and   return it to your mail box later the same
day when she is back on campus for History 480?

---

          is quite good at Exams, has good retention capacity, and would naturally not use any written course
material to answer the questions ... he is an honourable guy, former   '   , and a new   ?

If this is not possible, can he re-sit the Midterm at a later date if he is just too sick tomorrow?

I will speak to you tomorrow morning before your class.

Sincerely,

Appendix 5

Helen Brown

From: @aol.com
Sent: Tuesday, October 18, 2005 12:31 PM
To: Helen Brown
Subject: In class prsentation

Dear Dr. Brown,

It was a pleasure meeting you this morning.

          is going to take the rest of the week off.

He will approach you the beginning of November regarding the Exam Questions that you mentioned he might practice on for the Finals.

For the Thursday In-class Presentations [2 minutes each student] of their Research Reports,   will be summarizing hers for the class ... and we are wondering if   could also summarize   's as well??

In this way, at least this assignment will be finished and out of the way?

Thank you,

Appendix 6a

MEMO

To: Steve Lane and Dan Hawthorne
From: Helen Brown
Date: 19 October 2005
Attached: Two emails from parent

Re: History 476 Student's Parent

I received an email on October 18 from the parent of a student. I did not reply to the email, but when he arrived at my office with the student I asked the student to wait outside while I spoke privately to the parent. I told the parent I could not discuss a student with any third party. He responded by saying that there was no problem with that because he was the student's proxy and it is in their file. I replied that I had no documentation in regard to him. I then explained in the abstract, without reference to any particular student or any particular situation, what my general policy was in regard to mid-term exams missed for reasons of illness. The discussion was amicable and the parent left the building.

69

Appendix 6b

I next asked the student to come into my office. Since he appeared ill, I explained how I would deal with him not writing the mid-term that morning when it was scheduled. He made the decision not to write the exam and I supported that decision.

In the afternoon, I received a second email from the parent in regard to research presentations that my student and his sister, who is also in the class, are scheduled to make on Thursday. At that point I asked for a meeting with the Dean and also emailed the Chair of the History Department asking him to be present if possible.

I have never heard of a parent acting as proxy and whether such a thing exists at Malaspina or not, it is in my students' best interests that we deal directly with each other.

In regard to this specific case, I have not responded to the second email and will not have further communication with the parent.

Appendix 7a

SEP 1 3 2004

13 September, 2004   "Hand Delivered"

The Registrar
MALASPINA UNIVERSITY -COLLEGE
900 Fifth Street
Nanaimo, B.C.
V9R 5S5

543132
HXC: PROXY DAD   (SSEX)

RE: Student # 545-

Dear Registrar,

Would you kindly have in our student files that   Dad [   ] has
Proxy to speak on our behalf with respect to our Student Files at Malaspina University
College.

Since our dad is retired, he helps us keep track of our school records, course registrations,
and helps to search the Malaspina web page when we are busy.

Appendix 7b

It's particularly important that he have Proxy status because we may be busy with summer employment next year, or field placements, and it would be handy to have him with this access.

Thank you,

Signed:

| | , Student # 545- | |

This is Exhibit " A " referred to in the affidavit of *DARREL HANSBERGER*
sworn before me at *NANA* , *B.C.*
this *19* day of *JANUARY* 20-*09*

A Commissioner for taking affidavits
within the Province of British Columbia

72

Appendix 8a

Patrick Ross

From: Steve Lane
Sent: Wednesday, November 30, 2005 4:10 PM
To: Patrick Ross
Cc: Helen Brown
Subject:

Patrick,

Remember that parent who has tried to exercise a right of "proxy" over his two children?

Helen Brown of the History department came to see me this afternoon with a progress report on the kids. It looks like they didn't follow the instructions for their term paper assignments. She hasn't graded them yet, but no matter what the outcome, she expects she will be challenged on the grades. We fully expect the two students will appeal their grades for her course, in any event.

73

Appendix 8b

Helen is also worried about the father showing up in a belligerent, threatening manner again when the papers are returned. I believe she has good reason to be concerned.

I want to know if there's anything we can do proactively to deal with this situation?

Any advice or direction would be appreciated.

Thanks,

Steve

Steven M. Lane, Dean
Arts & Humanities
Malaspina University-College
900 Fifth Street
Nanaimo, BC
CANADA V9R 5S5
phone: (250) 740-6181
e-mail: lanes@mala.bc.ca

This is Exhibit " C " referred to in the
affidavit of ...... PATRICK ROSS ......
sworn before me at ...... NANAIMO ...... B.C.
this ... day of ... JANUARY ... 20 .09.
....
A Commissioner for taking Affidavits
within the Province of British Columbia

74

Appendix 9

As cited in a memo dated 21 November, 2007 "this guy" [turns out to be Patrick Ross, the vice-president of student services] confirmed this interaction:

Leslie Bishop

From: Leslie Bishop
Sent: Wednesday, November 21, 2007 11:28 AM
To: Leslie Bishop
Subject: - Nov. 19, 2007

* Holly called and indicated   was on campus again.

* I attended and told him to leave the campus (parking Lot D). He grumbled, called me a "moron" and left the car.

Appendix 10a

IN THE MATTER OF THE *HUMAN RIGHTS CODE*
R.S.B.C. 1996, C. 210 (AS AMENDED)

AND IN THE MATTER of a complaint before the
British Columbia Human Rights Tribunal

BETWEEN:

COMPLAINANT

AND:

MALASPINA UNIVERSITY COLLEGE, VANCOUVER ISLAND UNIVERSITY and
PATRICK ROSS

RESPONDENTS

Appendix 10b

"This guy" [Patrick Ross, the vice-president of student services] outright lied under oath came in his deposition to the British Columbia Human Rights Department where he stated:

16.   On or about November 19, 2007, I received a telephone call from the Malaspina Registration Centre advising that the Complainant was on campus waiting in a car in Parking Lot D. I attended at Parking Lot D and told the Complainant to leave the campus. Attached to this my Affidavit and marked as Exhibit "M" is a true copy of a November 21, 2007 memorandum my assistant, Leslie Bishop, drafted relating to my November 19, 2007 confrontation with the Complainant. At no time did I "bang on" the Complainant's window as alleged in the Complaint or otherwise threaten the Complainant.

SWORN BEFORE ME at the City of   )
Nanaimo, Province of British Columbia   )
this 14th day of January, 2009.   )
)
_____   )   _____
)   Patrick Ross
A Commissioner for taking Affidavits   )
for British Columbia   )
)

As such, Patrick Ross, the vice-president of student services apparently committed perjury – isn't that what it's called when one lies under oath?

Appendix 11

From: Darrel Mansbridge
Sent: Thursday, May 31, 2007 5:38 PM
To: Patrick Ross
Cc: Leslie Bishop
Subject: FW:

Pat,

Do you want me involved in this?

Darrel

This is Exhibit " K " referred to in the
affidavit of ... *PATRICK ROSS* ...
sworn before me at ... *NANAIMO, B.C.*
this ... day of ... *January* ... 20 *09*.

A Commissioner for taking Affidavits
within the Province of British Columbia

From: Leslie Petersen
Sent: Wednesday, May 30, 2007 11:37 AM
To: Patrick Ross; Darrel Mansbridge
Cc: Leslie Bishop; Hollis Lawson; Fred Jacklin
Subject:

Hi Darrel and Patrick,

Both yesterday and today, _____ has presented himself at the Registration Centre to accompany his son. Today, he became more aggressive in his tone and demeanor. While the Registration Centre staff are aware that _____ is not welcome on campus, none of the staff feel comfortable advising him of this fact. As a result of his presence today, the staff will be writing up an incidence report. Today, he attempted to go through the small barrier door and come around the counter. Because of our temporary location, neither myself or Fred are readily available to ask _____ to abide by the conditions of the letter.

If _____ presents himself again at the Registration Centre, they would rather call Security than confront him. Would it be worthwhile to remind him, either by telephone or in writing, of the conditions outlined in the previous letter? As he has been on campus recently, he has become emboldened again. Perhaps a reminder would be in order to prevent an escalation of his visits to campus?

Leslie Petersen
Admissions Manager
Malaspina University-College
petersenl@mala.bc.ca
(250) 740-6355

78

Appendix 12

FINAL RESEARCH PAPER

Childhood War Memories are Different for
Male and Female Children because of the Scripts
They Learned during Gender Development,
and the War Mothers that Cared for Them

Submitted To:
Dr. Helen Brown
History 476: Modern Childhood

Date Due/Submitted:
24 November, 2005